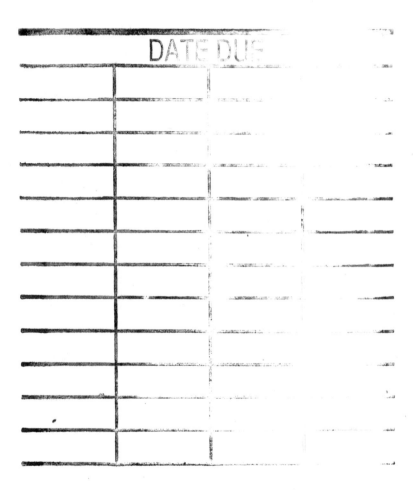

DATE DUE

DOWN CUT SHIN CREEK

Down Cut Shin Creek

The PACK HORSE LIBRARIANS of KENTUCKY

KATHI APPELT & JEANNE CANNELLA SCHMITZER

HarperCollins *Publishers*

To Clara Mounce—librarian, horsewoman,
friend—with love

K.A.

To Grace

J.C.S.

The photographs in this book are reproduced by permission of photographer Ann W. Olson (page vi); *The Courier-Journal*, Louisville, Kentucky (pages 30, 52); the Franklin D. Roosevelt Library, Hyde Park, New York (pages 5, 6, 34, 41); the Kentucky Historical Society, Frankfort, Kentucky (pages 2, 11, 28); the Mallie Cody Turner Collection, Morehead State University, Morehead, Kentucky (pages 4, 23, 42, 48); the National Archives and Records Administration, College Park, Maryland (pages 16, 20, 24, 32, 36, 45, 46, 50); and Western Kentucky University, Bowling Green, Kentucky (pages 10, 55).

The photographs on all other pages are part of the Work Projects Administration photographic collection, Public Records Division, Kentucky Department for Libraries and Archives.

Down Cut Shin Creek:
The Pack Horse Librarians of Kentucky
Copyright © 2001 by Kathi Appelt and Jeanne Cannella Schmitzer

Library of Congress Cataloging-in-Publication Data
Appelt, Kathi, date
   Down Cut Shin Creek : the pack horse librarians of Kentucky / Kathi Appelt & Jeanne Cannella Schmitzer.
     p.   cm.
   Includes bibliographical references.
   ISBN 0-06-029135-4 — ISBN 0-06-029244-X (lib. bdg.)
   1. Packhorse librarians—Kentucky—Juvenile literature.   2. Rural libraries—Kentucky—Juvenile literature.   3. Depressions—1929—Kentucky—Juvenile literature.   4. Mountain life—Kentucky—Juvenile literature.   5. Kentucky—Rural conditions—Juvenile literature.   6. United States. Works Progress Administration. Kentucky—Juvenile literature.   [1. Packhorse librarians—Kentucky.   2. Rural libraries—Kentucky.   3. Depressions—1929.   4. Mountain life—Kentucky.   5. Kentucky—History.   6. United States. Works Progress Administration. Kentucky.]   I. Schmitzer, Jeanne Cannella.   II. Title.
Z716.15 .A66   2001
027.0769'09173'4—dc21
                                                                                                          00-059702
                                                                                                                CIP
                                                                                                                 AC

Typography by Barbara Balch
   2   3   4   5   6   7   8   9   10
❖
First Edition

ACKNOWLEDGMENTS

The path this project took us along was often just as torturous as those steep byways taken by the pack horse librarians. We could never have reached our journey's end without the help of numerous people.

First, and foremost, we give heartfelt thanks to former pack horse librarian Grace Caudill Lucas, of Beattyville, Kentucky, who graciously allowed these two strangers into her home and told us about her life. We are indebted as well to Margaret Allen and her daughter, Heather Allen, for making our visit so memorable and welcome. Carrie Lynch, you contributed a wealth of information. Thank you!

More than once we were given able assistance by a host of librarians. We would particularly like to thank Tim Tingle and Jane Julian, Kentucky Department for Libraries and Archives; Nancy Snedeker, the Franklin D. Roosevelt Library; Eugene Morris, the National Archives; Clara Keyes, the Camden-Carroll Library at Morehead State University; Betty Carter, Department of Library Science, Texas Women's University; Jeannette Shouse and Raymond Moore, Breathitt County Public Library; Alice L. Birney, the Library of Congress; Jonathan Jeffrey, Special Collections, Western Kentucky University; Sharon Bidwell, *The Courier-Journal*, Louisville; Mary E. Winter, Kentucky Historical Society; and Sonya Spencer, Lee County Public Library.

We had many other folks who lent their support, encouragement, and time. They include George Ella Lyon, Debbie Leland, Donna Cooner, Elizabeth Neeld, Kathy Whitehead, and Ann W. Olson.

We have to give a big thank-you to Jacob Appelt, whose ninth-grade research project led to the authors' discovery of each other via the World Wide Web—it pays to help your children with their homework!

Marilyn Marlow of Curtis Brown kept the lanterns lit as we stumbled along.

This book would never have happened without the enthusiasm and loving guidance of our editor, Meredith Charpentier, whose belief in the project held us in good stead over the years it took us to find the trail's end. Thanks also go to her assistant, Marisa Miller, who has an uncanny knack for tying up loose strings.

And finally, both of us want to thank our husbands, Ken and Bill, who kept the home fires burning while we gallivanted across Kentucky, retracing the paths of the book women.

Thank you kindly, one and all!

—K.A. and J.C.S.

Grace Caudill Lucas, former pack horse librarian, fall 1999.

PUTTING WOMEN TO WORK

"Son, the times they was so hard, you couldn't hardly crack them."

GRACE CAUDILL LUCAS

They were the darkest of times, the years following the crash of the stock market in 1929. Thousands of people across the United States were cast out of their jobs, off their farms, out of their homes and apartments, and into the crushing depths of poverty. Fathers, forced out of work, abandoned their families rather than watch them suffer; mothers died of malnutrition; children went without shoes or shelter or schooling. An entire nation, it seemed, was standing in one long breadline, desperate for even the barest essentials. It was a crisis of monumental proportions. It was known as the Great Depression.

Already one of the poorest states in the country, Kentucky was particularly hard hit, especially the rocky and mountainous eastern half of the state. Coal was Kentucky's main resource. With so many factories shut down nationwide, and the use of natural gas for heating on the increase, the need for coal diminished and hundreds of mines were closed. Thousands of coal workers were laid off. Though tough and resilient by nature, many Kentuckians barely hung on.

To add to the despair, the Ohio River, which borders Kentucky, flooded in 1930, killing more than a hundred people and washing

This Kentucky girl's clothing shows the extreme poverty that many mountain people experienced during the 1930s.

away the already thin layer of topsoil that covered the hardscrabble landscape, making farming virtually impossible.

In 1933, Federal Emergency Relief Director Harry Hopkins sent Lorena Hickock, a former reporter for the *Minneapolis Tribune*, to report on the conditions in the area. She wrote back: "[Residents] live in abandoned mining camps. The rest live in little communities, rather like Indian villages—and without any kind of sanitation whatever—back up at the headwaters of creeks, in the mountains. . . . [F]ive babies up one of those creeks died of starvation in the last ten days. . . . [M]et an old woman half dead from pellegra [a skin disease caused by malnutrition], stumbling along on bare, gnarled old feet, begging for food."

President Franklin D. Roosevelt had to find a way to help the American people. In 1933, he created a relief program known as the New Deal. Two years later, he expanded the New Deal by adding the Works Progress Administration, which in 1939 was renamed the Work *Projects* Administration. The goals of the WPA were twofold: to put people to work and to promote social and cultural awareness with art, theater, and literature.

Many of the original New Deal programs required heavy physical labor. WPA workers built hundreds of schools, health clinics, roads, park facilities, and community centers. Much of what we now call our "infrastructure"—highways, schools, power plants, etc.—is here thanks to thousands of WPA workers. Most of those projects were considered "men's work," and even though today it is not unusual for women to work in these jobs, in the 1930s it was considered unseemly.

By 1935, however, with so many women heading households and ending up on the relief rolls, it was clear that employment for them was essential. Thus a concerted effort was made to create jobs to put women to work and take them off the dole. The new jobs included work in

First Lady Eleanor Roosevelt was a great advocate of WPA programs that put women to work. In 1937, she visited West Liberty, Kentucky, where she met with one of the pack horse librarians.

health services, school lunch programs, sewing projects, and libraries.

It was during the time of the WPA that many areas of the country, particularly poor rural areas, received free public library service for the very first time. Without a system of paved roads, reaching many of these areas required ingenuity. For example, in the backwaters of Mississippi and Louisiana, librarians delivered books on small flatboats that they navigated with poles through the marshy bayous.

The WPA sponsored other traveling libraries. In the marshes of Louisiana, books were delivered by flatboat.

But it was eastern Kentucky's Pack Horse Library Project that proved to be the most innovative of all.

AN ORDINARY DAY

(THE WAY IT MIGHT HAVE BEEN)

It's early, four thirty A.M., and the air in the dark barn is cold and crisp. In the dim light of the coal-oil lamp, the book woman can see gray puffs of steam float from her horse's nostrils. She shivers. At the age of twenty-two, and having grown up in these hills, she knows how bitterly cold a January day here can get.

As she brushes the gelding's black coat, she wishes she could stay home, close to her two young children still asleep in the tiny wood-frame house nestled on the side of the hill. Her mother will keep an eye on them for her, but she will miss her babes and worry about them nonetheless.

She checks her saddlebags. They're filled with tattered books and magazines, a few bulletins from the WPA, some reference materials, and a couple of homemade scrapbooks, one she made herself and one sent by a Girl Scout troop all the way from Cincinnati. She pats the horse's neck, then leads him to the gate, where she tightens the girth on the saddle and pulls herself onto his back.

These carriers begin their day at dawn along Cut Shin Creek.

The rugged terrain provided tough footing for both mount and rider.

Kentucky is known for its fine thoroughbred racehorses, horses that are worth more than the book woman will earn in her entire lifetime. But to her, none of them are worth as much as this one. She leases the horse from her neighbor for fifty cents a week plus feed. Surefooted and gentle, this is a horse she can rely upon to get her across the rocky mountain slopes they will travel today. The two of them are partners in the truest sense.

Slowly she makes her way out of the yard and looks up. There are no stars in the pitch-black sky. She knows they are being blocked by heavy clouds, a sure sign of worse weather to come, probably snow, most certainly freezing rain. She pulls her thin coat tighter around her neck. It will be a long day for the book woman and her trusted steed.

Most parts of the trail are lonely and quiet, especially in the winter.

She urges her mount steadily along, up and down stony hillsides. At one particularly steep rise, she dismounts and leads him. "No point in taking a spill," she says. She goes slowly so that he won't stumble and take both of them down. At the top of the rise, she remounts.

She whistles as they go, old tunes that she has known all her life. The horse nods his head in rhythm to the gospel sound.

One of her first stops is at a house where the husband has been wounded by a gunshot. She knows how it happened, as there aren't many secrets in these hills. He's a moonshiner.

Moonshining, the illegal distilling and selling of "corn likker," or whiskey, is a full-blown industry here. She doesn't judge the people who are engaged in it. It's a living, after all. But the people doing it take

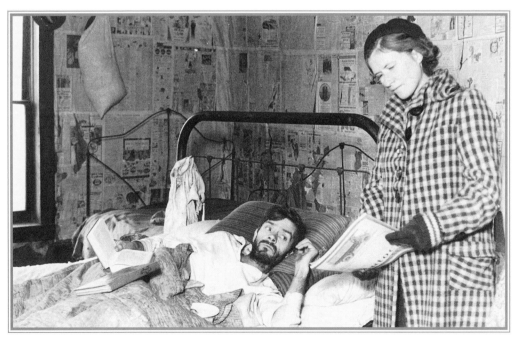

Neighbor helping neighbor was at the root of the Pack Horse Library Project.

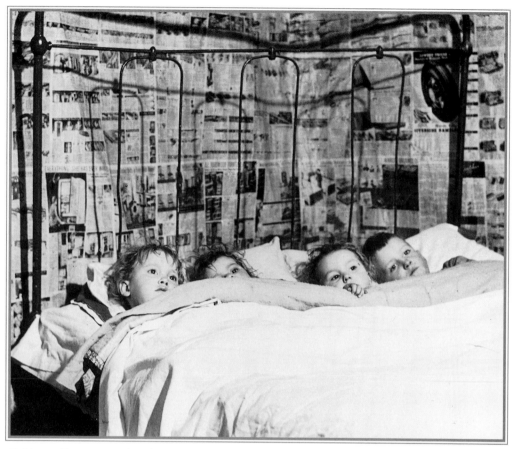

Cabin walls were insulated against the cold with newspaper, but often that wasn't enough.

great risks. Not only is it against the law, but the competition is fierce.

Some of the worst fights and feuds occur between rival moonshiners, with their scuffles often ending in gunshot wounds or worse, death. The man in this cabin is barely hanging on. Today she has brought his wife some magazines: an old copy of *Life* and a newer issue of *Women's Home Companion*. She has also brought a Sunday-school pamphlet for their small children, huddled under the covers atop a small pallet in the corner of the room. All she can see are the tops of their heads. They don't say a word.

"Can't tell you how much we appreciate it," the wife tells her, and hands her the magazines from her previous visit.

The book woman doesn't stay long. The inside of the cabin is not much warmer than the outside, and there are many miles left to go.

The morning is slipping by as the book woman approaches one of her favorite stops, Monica School, a one-room schoolhouse where her best friend, Carrie, is the teacher. There are forty-five students here who will share the few books that she brings to them. She also brings reference books—a health book and a book about weather—that the school so direly needs.

Before she gets to the stoop, the door bursts open and a tall blond boy with sparkling eyes and a chipped front tooth grins at her.

"We been a-waitin' for you, book lady," he says. "We done read every one of the books you left last time." Then he grabs the reins and ties her horse to the front rail. The boy is one of her favorites. She has known his family all her life, and his mama was a great friend during those first days after her husband left and she thought her heart would break in two.

She pats the boy and asks about her friend. "Mama's doin' fine, miss," he says. Then he takes her saddlebags and leads the way into the schoolhouse.

She smiles when she realizes that she has a copy of *Robinson Crusoe* in her saddlebags. It's one of the children's favorites. They also love poetry, and she tries to see to it that there is at least one volume to give them every two weeks when she makes her stop. She has lent them a copy of Robert Louis Stevenson's *A Child's Garden of Verses* so many times that many of the children can recite it by heart. There are never enough books to go around. She wishes she could hand each child his or her own book, but there is always a shortage.

Most of the schools in eastern Kentucky are like this one: small one-room affairs made of logs; they open in July and close toward the latter part of February, only a month away. Then the children here will help their families with the spring planting.

The book woman knows there are many children in these hills, like the moonshiner's little ones, who do not attend school at all, and more than once she has been asked to stop and read to families where no one can make out the words. Even though they can't read, they still ask for the books, especially those with pictures.

The forty-five children in Monica School are lucky, despite the poor conditions. Their teacher is dedicated, and the school is heated by a coal-burning stove. As the book woman unpacks her saddlebags, she is able to warm herself a little. Then she pulls out a tattered copy of *The Little Shepherd of Kingdom Come*, a novel about the Civil War by Kentucky author John Fox, Jr. She will have time to read only one chapter, but she leaves the book for the teacher to finish over the next two weeks, when she will return.

Too soon, she waves good-bye and climbs back onto her horse. The towheaded boy hands her the saddlebags. Then he reaches into his pockets and lifts out two large walnuts and hands them to her. She doesn't want to take them. Most likely they are the boy's lunch, but it would be wrong to refuse them. As if he's reading her thoughts, he

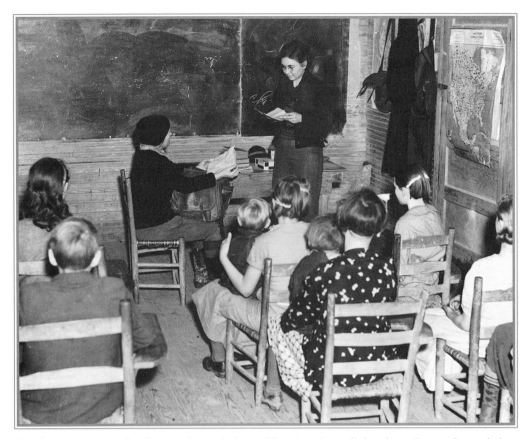

To this one-room schoolhouse the pack horse librarian (seated) has brought much-needed reference materials for the students.

says, "Don't worry, I got me a whole passel of these. Mama sent them with me this mornin'," he assures her. "We got that big walnut tree right by the woodshed, 'member?"

She pictures his family place, with its tidy yard and a few chickens, and even a climbing rose beside the porch. "Yep," she admits, "there is a walnut tree, all right." She cups the walnuts in her hand and thanks him. It is beginning to drizzle, and the warmth that she felt inside the schoolhouse quickly gives way to the icy rain. She must hurry.

Students say good-bye to the book woman and her mule. WPA workers built this school in Hindman, Kentucky.

❧♛❧

The weather is getting worse. The freezing rain stings her face, and the book woman pulls her collar up as high as it will go. The rain has slowed her down, and she knows that Mrs. Stuart will be waiting for her at the arbor just ahead. She urges her horse to step up his pace.

Mrs. Stuart lives nine miles off the book woman's route, in a small community with five other families. Every two weeks she walks the nine miles to meet the book woman, carrying the heavy books in a cloth sack and exchanging them for new ones, which she'll share with the other families.

The book woman hopes that the weather prevented Mrs. Stuart from making her treacherous journey, but as she rounds the bend, she hears the tiny woman singing at the top of her lungs. The book woman smiles and joins in. It's an old hymn that she's known since she was a little girl.

Pack horse librarians traveled year-round through all kinds of weather.

This woman sits by the wood stove enjoying a book brought by a pack horse librarian.

As she reaches the brushy arbor, which gives them a small amount of protection from the wind, the song makes her feel just a little warmer.

"Didn't think you'd come today," announces the book woman, "what with this weather and all."

Mrs. Stuart laughs and pats the horse's neck. "What, and miss a chance to get me a good visit with the relatives?"

The book woman has to laugh too. During the summer months,

the brush arbor serves as a chapel where Sunday meetings take place. It's right beside an old graveyard. Many of the headstones have dates that go back to the Revolutionary War. There are plenty of Stuarts there.

The two women exchange books and say their farewells. Now there is only one more stop. "Just a few more miles," she assures her horse. But she doesn't remind him that they will be the day's hardest miles yet.

The sleet is coming down faster now, making it hard for the book woman to see ahead of her. She relies on the horse to find their way. Her hands are so cold, she can't feel her fingers, and her back aches from the many miles they've already come. The last stop is near, and just a mile or so from there is her own cozy house, warmer because of her little ones. Thinking about them makes her yearning to be home that much keener. But right now it feels as if home is in another county.

She hurries her horse along. She can't go too much faster, though, because the ground is slippery. Every so often the horse slides. She hangs on with her frozen fingers. If she had an accident out here alone, it might be a long time before someone came for her. She could easily freeze to death in the meantime. The day is rapidly getting darker. It must be around three P.M., she reckons. It feels much later.

At last, she can smell the smoke from the cabin ahead. It stings her nostrils as she guides her horse to the side of the house. There's a new window—not one with glass panes, but a wooden one that swings out. She taps on it. The tapping brings on a flash of pain through her frozen hand. She shakes it and then tucks it beneath her armpit, trying to warm it up a bit.

The window opens a tiny crack.

"Didn't want you to open the door," she says. "Might let in too much cold."

"Thanks," says the young woman behind the window. Her name is Eldora, and she's barely fifteen and getting ready to have her second child. The first one died of scarlet fever. Eldora almost died too.

"How're you comin' along?" asks the book woman.

"Just a couple weeks to go now," replies Eldora.

The book woman has brought her some "doctor books," books about child rearing and giving birth. Eldora reaches out and takes them.

"Wait a minute," she says as she pulls the window shut. The book woman is anxious to go, but she waits. The horse stomps his front foot. The book woman knows that she can't let him stand still for too long, or he'll begin to seize up. She walks him in a circle around the yard.

The window opens again. "Here you go!" Eldora hollers, holding a slip of paper out in her hand. The book woman rides up to the window again.

"It's my granny's receipt for rice pudding. It's easy to make." The book woman takes the paper and slips it into her pocket.

"Well, I'll say. You tell your granny thank you. There's nothin' I

Generally log cabins in Kentucky's Cumberland Mountains had no windows—the door was left open year-round for light and ventilation.

don't love so much as rice pudding." Thinking about the sweet dessert reminds the book woman that she's had nothing to eat since breakfast, almost twelve hours ago.

She waves good-bye. Maybe there will be a healthy new baby here next time she stops by. She says three small prayers. One for Eldora and her baby. Another for her own children. And finally, she says, "Lord, keep a watch over me and this horse. I'm a-countin' on you to lead us home."

As she rides down the last hill that leads toward the creek, the rain finally slows down. Her wet coat is stiff with ice. Once home, she will have to hang it on a peg near the stove, but it will still take a couple of days for it to completely dry out. With the ceasing of the rain, quietness fills the air. It's soothing, and she looks up for the first time in hours. The sky is still leaden with heavy gray clouds. There will be more bad weather soon.

The quiet is interrupted with a new sound, a roar. There's a catch in her throat. Only one thing makes that sound—the creek when it's full. Normally, Cut Shin Creek is only a few inches deep, and she and the horse splash across it in just a few paces. But as she comes down the hill, she can see that it is over its banks, lapping over the bottoms of the maple trees along its side.

She pulls the horse up and takes it all in. Her house is only a mile or so beyond this creek. The only other way to get home would be to retrace the route, all twenty miles. She would have to stop at Eldora's for the night, which would mean taking a meal there. Eldora and her young husband barely have enough for themselves.

"Let's get on home," she tells the horse. The horse seems to agree, and without hesitating, he slips into the rushing creek. It's not as deep as she thought, the water only up to the horse's belly. But as they cross, the horse splashes the chilly water up onto her legs, and it soaks through her pants. She catches her breath as the cold water drenches her shoes. Her teeth begin to chatter. A minute later, they're across.

Fording Cut Shin Creek: Kentucky's mountains had few roads and fewer bridges. Cut Shin Creek was supposedly named when a timberman cut himself with his ax.

The horse knows they are close to home, and he picks up his pace. The trail from the creek is worn and familiar. They head up the hill and then down again. It is five P.M. and almost completely dark.

At last, she enters her small yard. Jones, her redbone hound, crawls out from under the house to greet her as she dismounts. A bolt of pain surges through her calves as her frozen feet touch the rocky ground. She's not sure she can even walk on them, and so she slowly places one in front of the other as she leads the horse and Jones into the dark barn. This morning, before she left, the barn felt cold, but now it feels as warm as the equator. She pulls off her glove and pats the hound standing beside her whining. His fur is warm to her touch.

The horse stamps his foot, and she loosens the girth and then pulls off his saddle. She has to work quickly to keep him from cooling down too fast. She drapes an old blanket over him and pours a bucket of corn into his trough. After her own dinner, she will bring him a bowl of warm mash and rub him down.

But now she walks out of the barn, Jones at her side, and hurries into the house, into the arms of her little ones and her own mother. The book woman is home at last. Her job is done.

Tomorrow she will ride the horse into town, where she will meet with the other librarians for their weekly reports. She will not have anything unusual to report. She is, after all, an ordinary woman, doing what she can to make life a little better for herself and her family.

She's just doing what she can.

One reason the Pack Horse Library Project was successful was that the carriers were local people. These women would have been familiar faces to the folks along their route.

NO PAVED ROADS

Thousands of people lived in the crooks and hollows of Kentucky's mountains. Without newspapers, telephones, or radios, they were almost totally isolated from the outside world. Since there were no paved or even gravel roads, the only way in was by foot, horse, or mule.

People followed creek beds and mountain paths to their tiny communities and homes in the hollows. Small one-room schoolhouses, nestled in coves and mining camps, were almost entirely removed from the outside world. With the exception of that provided by a few private and church institutions, library service was nonexistent, especially to those outside the large cities.

By the late 1920s, some other states with isolated rural populations began to serve their residents with bookmobiles. The lack of roads in eastern Kentucky made this impossible. The small one-room schoolhouses that sat in remote mountain communities barely had enough textbooks for their students, let alone libraries. Some had no books at all. The problem seemed overwhelming.

This bookmobile served the people in Thomas County, Washington.

A cabin deep in the backwoods of the Cumberland Mountains.

In the face of daunting essential needs—food, clothing, medicine, employment—funding for libraries seemed a very low priority. Without enough money to feed their bodies, how in the world could money be found to "feed their minds"? asked First Lady Eleanor Roosevelt.

The answer came in the form of an ingenious WPA program known as the Kentucky Pack Horse Library Project.

WHO THEY WERE

The way it worked was simple: The WPA paid the salaries for the librarians to maintain a headquarters library, usually at the county seat, and to carry books on horseback throughout the county. Their circuits were worked out so that new books were dropped off at Center 1, the books already there were taken on to Center 2, and so on. A center might be a school, a community center, a post office, or even a home.

The Kentucky pack horse librarians were tough. They had to be in order to travel atop horses and mules over the rockiest terrain, through all kinds of weather, carrying books and magazines up and down creek beds named Hell-for-Sartin, Troublesome, and Cut Shin because of their treacherous natures.

The book women were dedicated. Although their salary was only twenty-eight dollars a month, they were proud of the work they did. Taking books to people who had never had access to them before was not only hard work, it was important work.

The people the librarians served in these isolated hills and hollows were their neighbors and friends. Most of them traced their ancestry back to the Revolutionary War, when their great-great-great-grandfathers were given parcels of land in return for their military service. The librarians wanted the same things their neighbors did—a better life, a better education, some knowledge of the outside world. Their dedication helped thousands of people achieve these goals.

They were determined. It took determination to overcome the obstacles—the difficult terrain, the wariness of their patrons toward "book larnin'," and especially the desperate shortage of reading materials that plagued the program from the start. The government did not pay for books or materials, or the centers in which they were housed, only the small monthly salaries of the librarians. The precious books came strictly from donations.

Some Kentuckians traced their heritage back to pre-Revolutionary War days, and their way of life remained almost unchanged well into the twentieth century.

Pack horse librarians were brave and determined.

The pack horse librarians were much like door-to-door salespeople, and even though they weren't selling anything, they did have to convince their neighbors to participate. The materials had to be carefully considered to prevent offending the conservative ways of the mountain residents. Magazines such as *Love Story* or *True Story*, or detective magazines that were considered "thrillers"—all of which were popular at the time—might have affronted some folks and turned them away from the program.

At one mountain home, a mother continued to decline to participate despite the best efforts of the carrier. Finally she relented, and the next time the carrier visited, the woman greeted her with warm enthusiasm. "They are all nice clean stories!" she said.

The pack horse librarians did nothing less than bring the modern world into the lives of their patrons.

That element of trust was instrumental in the success of the pack horse program. Here were neighbor women who knew the folks on their routes by name and understood the kinds of materials that they would enjoy.

The pack horse librarians were not "outlanders" coming in and trying to tell folks how to live or what to read!

Carriers provided their own horses and mules, but often walked parts of their routes as well.

INSIDE THE SADDLEBAGS

Magazines were far more popular than books, especially "practical" magazines such as *Women's Home Companion* and *Popular Mechanics*. The mountaineers were hungry for ways to improve their lives, and they found the magazines on home health care, cooking, agriculture, child care, parenting, canning, hygiene, hunting, and machinery particularly helpful.

Besides wanting practical information, the mountaineers also dreamed about life outside the mountains and were eager to read about foreign lands, which they discovered in the pages of *National Geographic*. They particularly enjoyed stories about the American west and found *Western Story Magazine* a real pleasure.

Many of the books the mountaineers liked to read are still popular today: *Rebecca of Sunnybrook Farm*, *Robinson Crusoe*, and *Gulliver's Travels*. Classic authors like Charles Dickens and William Shakespeare found new readers in Kentucky homes.

Always, children's books were in the greatest demand, and there

Children's books were always in high demand by both children and adults.

The carriers used a variety of containers for their materials—here a drawstring bag.

were never enough of them. And they weren't just for kids. Many adults who had never learned to read liked them because the pictures helped them figure out the stories. Sometimes, the children of the household read out loud to the adults and actually helped their parents and grandparents learn to read.

THUMMIN' AND DOG-EARS

After a month or so on the circuit, the books were brought back to the central headquarters by the carrier. There they were mended and cleaned, then transferred to another circuit. Each headquarters had between four and six carriers. The carriers went out three or four times a week, taking a different route each day, and then repeating those routes every two weeks. The routes were roughly eighteen miles long, so a pack horse librarian was used to traveling fifty to eighty miles each week. Once a week all the carriers met at the headquarters to write short reports and help mend and clean the books.

Keeping the materials in shape was no small undertaking. The books and magazines that came to the libraries weren't new. They were already used. Often they were discards from other libraries—books considered too worn out for those libraries to continue to circulate. Carrying these raggedy materials in saddlebags, string bags, pillowcases, and suitcases wore them down even more. But the heavy usage from the patrons was particularly damaging. "Thummin'" caused a great deal of wear and tear to books that were often already in poor condition when they arrived at the library. In a report sent to the WPA, one librarian wrote that she and her carriers had attacked the problem of dog-ears by making bookmarks out of old Christmas cards. These attracted so much attention among their clients that old Christmas cards were collected and given as rewards to children who

Each of the headquarters was staffed by a head librarian, who kept the materials well organized.

Head librarian Rose Farmer checks out books to one of the few men carriers in the Pack Horse Library Project.

returned their books promptly and in good condition. Since most of the children had never seen a Christmas card, the bookmarks became highly treasured prizes.

SOMETHING BACK IN RETURN

Early on, there was another problem faced by the pack horse libraries. Many of the mountain women they served felt uncomfortable taking something that was free, even though it was only on loan, without giving something back in return. So the women would often give the librarians their best recipes or a beloved family quilt pattern as a gesture of gratitude. One good turn deserved another.

Somewhere along the line, an enterprising carrier decided to take some of the recipes and quilt patterns, along with articles and stories from the more worn-out magazines, and paste them together in a scrapbook. The idea took root and became a common practice for all the pack horse libraries.

Two recipes found in one of the librarians' reports are for Ash Cake and Rice Pudding.

This young woman in Mill Creek, Kentucky, is expecting her first child and welcomes materials pertaining to hygiene, childbirth, and parenting.

ASH CAKE
(Recipe over 100 years old)

1 cup sour milk
1 teaspoon salt

Add meal until stiff.
Have hot wood ashes in fireplace and make hole in hot ashes, put in ash cake. Cover with hot coals and bake until brown.
THIS RECIPE WAS GIVEN BY MRS. GRANT OWENS, AGE SIXTY YEARS, WATTS CREEK, WALLINS, KENTUCKY, CIRCA 1939–43.

RICE PUDDING

2 cups cooked rice
1 cup sugar
2 eggs
½ teaspoon lemon extract
1 lump butter size of an egg
1 cup sour milk

Add pinch soda. Mix soda with milk, then add other mixture.
RECIPE BY MRS. REED, AGE SIXTY-TWO, MOLUS, KENTUCKY, CIRCA 1939–43.

Some of these scrapbooks actually went into circulation. Some of them became beloved treasures for the librarians themselves. There is one in the archives collection at the Franklin D. Roosevelt Library in Hyde Park, New York. It was most likely given as a gift to either the president or Mrs. Roosevelt.

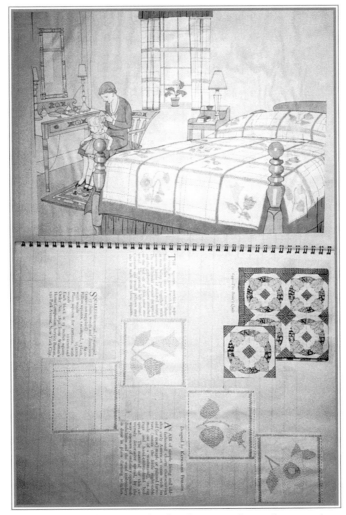

An example of the scrapbooks that were lovingly created by the pack horse librarians.

The pack horse librarians also carried with them religious pamphlets, old sermons, church bulletins, booklets on health care, cookbooks, and bulletins on first aid and household help. It seems that once the people in the mountains were sold on library service, they couldn't get enough to read.

MRS. NOFCIER'S PENNY FUND

Most of the libraries were started with a nucleus of two hundred to eight hundred books, all of which were donated from a wide variety of sources, including women's clubs, PTAs, schools, churches, and universities.

Eight hundred books seems like a lot until you consider that each pack horse library served between five and ten thousand people. That's about one book to share among every six to twelve people. It's easy to see that those early collections hardly began to meet the needs of everyone who wanted a book.

To help overcome the shortage, the pack horse program had a true champion in the person of Lena B. Nofcier, Chairman of Library Service for the Kentucky PTA.

An influential person, she argued for funds to support the program. "It is impossible for a teacher to conduct classes without books and other printed aids," she said in an address to an organization of Kentucky

Of all the obstacles facing the pack horse librarians, shortages of reading material were the hardest to overcome.

Mrs. Lena B. Nofcier.

teachers and parents. "After a child learns to read, he must have access to books." She further argued that "library service should be provided for *all* people, rural as well as urban, colored as well as white."

She approached PTAs around the state, pleading with them to donate books, magazines, and other materials. Boy Scout troops, Sunday-school classes, and children's school groups collected materials and sent them to local collection points.

Without question, the most successful fund-raising program was the establishment of the Penny Fund. Through the Penny Fund, Nofcier asked every PTA member in the state to give at least one penny with which to buy books for pack horse libraries. New children's books cost between $1.75 and $2.00 at the time, and the Penny Fund became a means of purchasing new books throughout the entire existence of the Pack Horse Library Project.

One of the most poignant letters that Nofcier received during this time was one from a small mountain school in Piner, Kentucky, with

A coal miner shares a book with his daughters before leaving for the night shift in a Nelson, Kentucky, mine.

$2.23 tucked into the envelope. "Please accept our little gift from our school children that it might make some other children happy to have some library books to read in their schools too." It was signed by Mr. Norton, the principal of Piner School, on January 11, 1937.

A SHINING JEWEL

The uniqueness of the Pack Horse Library Project stirred a lot of interest around the country. Articles appeared in *The New York Times*, *The Christian Science Monitor*, *Rural America*, and a host of other newspapers and magazines. In addition, the WPA itself saw in Kentucky's pack horse libraries a successful program, one that relied upon the local community and took people off the relief rolls.

It was not unusual for administrators in Washington, D.C., to tout the Kentucky program as a kind of "shining jewel" among the vast number of WPA projects. The dedication of the pack horse librarians in spite of every difficulty appealed to the American notion of toughness and patriotism; the idea that any obstacle could be overcome if people tried hard enough spoke deeply to the most basic sense of how the American people saw themselves.

And with great ingenuity, the pack horse librarians put to use almost every article that came their way. At their library headquarters

A Northerner en route to Florida stops off at Wooten, Kentucky, to drop off a trunkful of magazines and newspapers.

Pack horse librarian Rose Farmer stands by her display at a WPA conference in Indianapolis, Indiana.

you might have seen 3" x 15" cheese boxes used as card files. Prune boxes doubled as sorting boxes for incoming donations. License plates folded to a ninety-degree angle served well as bookends for the collection, and broom handles served as newspaper racks. One library used an auto jack as a book press for binding the collections of scrapbooks created from discards.

The pack horse libraries made recycling popular before the rest of us even knew what the term meant.

THIS GOOD WORK

Despite its problems, and the ongoing shortage of materials, the Pack Horse Library Project was considered a rousing success story. But success sometimes carried with it other problems. For instance, one family complained that their son's new nightly reading habits meant they had to purchase more lamp oil. Another parent allowed only a single book for all her children in order to prevent squabbles. And still another parent grew irate over the fact that he could not get his children to do their chores because all they wanted to do was sit and read.

Still, the benefits far outweighed the drawbacks. From the early beginnings of the program in 1935 in two counties, Leslie and Harlan, to the final years, when more than thirty counties were included, over 100,000 people participated in the Pack Horse Library Project. And where they did, the new library service almost certainly provided a meaningful escape from their troubles.

Unfortunately, the pack horse libraries did not last long. With the economy rebounding and World War II in full swing, the need for the government to put people to work waned. So in 1943, the project ended with the dismantling of the WPA. Without the WPA, pack

This carrier in Leslie County was always a welcome visitor.

horse libraries could no longer pay their workers, and one of the most well-liked rural outreach services was discontinued. However, even though the services themselves came to an end, their influence did not.

Most importantly, pack horse libraries instilled in many the love of reading. "The Pack Horse Library Project was the thing that really got the children interested in reading, and gave them a desire to read," insisted schoolteacher Carrie Lynch. Every mile traveled brought new ideas and fresh interests to people in isolated areas.

Wrote Gladys Lainhart, a young pack horse worker, in a letter to the Kenwick PTA in Lexington, Kentucky, in 1937, "It would be difficult to estimate how much this good work is doing to brighten the lives of the people in our Kentucky mountains."

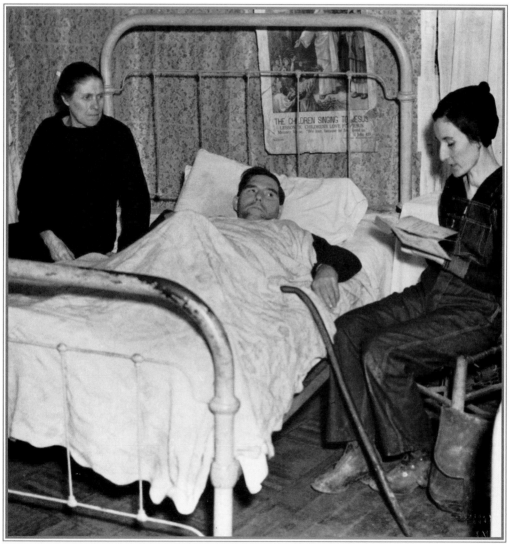

This pack horse librarian has gained the trust of a homebound man and his wife.

THE LEGACY

Between 1943, when pack horse library service ended, and 1957, when bookmobiles became more common, eastern Kentuckians were left with little library service, and many had none at all. County libraries, if they existed, struggled to keep their heads above water and could not even consider delivery or outreach.

Nothing matched the services provided by the Pack Horse Library Project, and it would be years before many areas had library service again.

It's not surprising that in 1956 it was a congressman from Kentucky, the late Carl D. Perkins, who would sponsor the Library Services Act that made the first federal appropriations for library service.

As a young man during the 1930s, Perkins was a teacher in rural Knott County. We know that the school in which he taught was serviced by one of Kentucky's book women, so it's highly possible that their dedication made an impact on his lifelong support for libraries, not only in Kentucky but in the whole country. The Library

United States Representative Carl D. Perkins was a strong advocate of public libraries.

Services Act (LSA) that he sponsored helped provide funds for the establishment of new libraries, the building of branch libraries, the purchase of bookmobiles, the procurement of library collections, and the hiring of new librarians. In short, the LSA helped build a system of libraries in our country that is among the world's best. Maybe, just maybe, a pack horse librarian helped inspire him. We'll never know for sure.

The fact remains that the project created a desire for reading and learning in all who participated. It operated in the most difficult terrain and under tremendous social pressures. And it created a usable collection of reading materials from ragged, unwanted donations.

The Kentucky Pack Horse Library Project and its book women deserve credit for their services, and acknowledgment for their part in library history—indeed in the very history of our country. What they gave to their constituents couldn't be measured in money, for what they gave was no less than the keys to the world.

Saddled up and ready to go!

BIBLIOGRAPHY

INTERVIEWS

Lucas, Grace Caudill. Interview by authors. Beattyville, Kentucky, May 31, 1998.

Lynch, Carrie. Interview by authors. Beattyville, Kentucky, June 17, 1998.

BOOKS

Blakey, George T. *Hard Times and New Deal in Kentucky: 1929–1939*. Lexington, Ky.: University Press of Kentucky, 1986.

Caudill, Harry M. *Night Comes to the Cumberlands: A Biography of a Depressed Area*. Boston: Little, Brown and Company, 1963.

ARTICLES, PAMPHLETS, AND ORIGINAL SOURCE MATERIAL

Beach, Robert. "Book-Extension Services in Eastern Kentucky." *Mountain Life and Work*, Vol. 17, No. 12 (Summer 1941): 1–8, 18.

Chapman, Edward A. "WPA and Rural Libraries." *Bulletin of the American Library Association*, Vol. 32, No. 10 (October 1, 1938): 703–8.

Comstock, Sarah. "Byways of Library Work." *Outlook*, Vol. 106 (January 24, 1914): 200–5.

Coode, Thomas H., and John F. Bauman. "Dear Mr. Hopkins: A New Dealer Reports from Eastern Kentucky." *Register of the Kentucky Historical Society*, Vol. 78 (Winter 1980): 59.

Crawford, Byron. "'Book Women' Brought Hope to Isolated Kentuckians." Louisville *Courier-Journal* (November 5, 1995).

———. "A Great Stone Face, Berried Treasure, Taps for Spike—and More." Louisville *Courier-Journal* (April 24, 1996).

———. "The Times Were Tough, but Book Woman Was Tougher." Louisville *Courier-Journal* (December 17, 1995).

Edwards, Dorothy. "The Romance of Kentucky Libraries." *Wilson Library Bulletin*, Vol. 17, No. 4 (December 1942): 293–95.

"Harlan County's 'Book Woman' Hitchhikes." Louisville *Courier-Journal* (August 23, 1936).

"Just What Is a Pack Horse Library?" Records of the Works Progress Administration, Record Group 69. National Archives, Washington, D.C., date unknown.

"Libraries." Pamphlet, Works Progress Administration. Franklin D. Roosevelt Library Archives, Hyde Park, New York. Date unknown.

"Looking Back: 50 Years Ago . . . WPA Library Projects in Kentucky." *Kentucky Libraries*, Vol. 53 (Spring 1985): 28–29.

"Mounted Library, a Relief Project." *The New York Times* (May 8, 1935).

"Notes on Traveling Libraries—Kentucky." Records of the Works Progress Administration, Record Group 69. National Archives, Washington, D.C., date unknown.

"Pack Horse Libraries in Kentucky." Records of the Works Progress Administration, Record Group 69. National Archives, Washington, D.C., date unknown.

"Pack Horse Library: A Kentucky W.P.A. Project." *Rural America* (October 1939): 11–12.

Rhodenbaugh, Beth. "Book Women Started in Kentucky." Louisville *Courier-Journal* (December 11, 1938).

Roosevelt, Eleanor. "What Libraries Mean to the Nation." *Bulletin of the American Library Association*, Vol. 30, No. 6 (June 1936): 477.

Schmitzer, Jeanne Cannella. "Reaching Out to the Mountains: The Pack Horse Library of Eastern Kentucky." *Register of the Kentucky Historical Society*, Vol. 95, No. 1 (Winter 1997): 57–77.

State Librarian Historical Sketches, 1923–1946, Box 1. Kentucky Department for Libraries and Archives, Frankfort, Ky.

State Librarian Official Correspondence, 1932–1960, Boxes 28 and 29. Kentucky Department for Libraries and Archives, Frankfort, Ky.

Townsend, Rev. G. W. "Book Women Carry Culture to Eastern Kentucky Hills." *In Kentucky* (Winter 1939): 38.

Woodward, Ellen S. "WPA Library Projects." *Wilson Library Bulletin*, Vol. 12 (April 1938): 518–20.

———. "The Lasting Values of WPA." Works Progress Administration Papers, Record Group 69, Series 737, Box 8. National Archives, Washington, D.C., date unknown.

WPA in Kentucky Records. Box 309. Kentucky Department for Libraries and Archives, Frankfort, Ky.

"WPA Travelling Libraries." Works Progress Administration Papers, Record Group 69, Series 743, Box 1. National Archives, Washington, D.C., date unknown.

THESES

McElroy, Lucy B. "The Works Progress Administration Library Extension Project in the Mountain Counties of Kentucky." Texas Women's University, Denton, Tex., May 1995.

Schmitzer, Jeanne C. "The Pack Horse Library Project of Eastern Kentucky: 1936–1943." University of Tennessee, Knoxville, Tenn., December 1998.

WEBSITES

Franklin D. Roosevelt Library and Museum:
    http://www.fdrlibrary.marist.edu
Kentucky Department for Libraries and Archives:
    http://www.kdla.state.ky.us
Kentucky Historical Society:
    http://kentuckyhistory.org
Library of Congress:
    http://lcweb.loc.gov
New Deal Network:
    http://newdeal.feri.org

INDEX

References to photographs appear in *italics*.